Praise for SUSAN O'BRIEN

I have worked with Susan O'Brien and her team for several years, and over that time have assisted her with dozens of her clients who are engaged in complex, high net worth estate planning.

Each client project is complex; it involves fact gathering and goal identification before my involvement commences, and then a course of multiple meetings and steps with her team, the client, myself, and other allied professionals.

Susan and her team are always prepared and do full and detailed work ups. They quarterback the process and have never, not once, dropped the ball. Each project has been brought to successful completion. Each client was fully supported and comfortable at each stage along the way. That is a truly impressive track record. I work with a variety of advisory teams in similar circumstances, and I can honestly say that none of those teams have performed at the same high level.

John Poyser
Partner, Tradition Law
Author of Capacity and Undue Influence
Co-author of ten editions of The Taxation of Trusts

I have grown to deeply appreciate Susan's approachable, reliable, learned, and trusted professional services, as have several of her clients who subsequently engaged with the Calgary Foundation to advance their philanthropic objectives.

A continuous learner, a respected Calgarian, a recognizable face in the crowd, and yet, a humble leader, Susan believes that which is emulated by renowned author and visionary leader Simon Sinek: "People don't buy what you do; they buy why you do it."

With gratitude, Susan, for all your contributions and dedication!

Laily Pirbhai

Vice president, Donor Engagement, Calgary Foundation

I asked Susan years ago how many clients she had. She gave me a number. I asked her how many A clients she had. She gave me the same number. Lesson learned. Every client is important to Susan and A New Way Forward for Wealth Management *is a compilation of her years of wisdom and insight that should be a must-read to help you reach your wealth management goals.*

Leo Pusateri

President and founder, Pusateri Consulting and the Sabbatical Experience
Author of Mirror Mirror on the Wall Am I the Most Valued of them All?

Passion, knowledge, and a genuine interest in achieving the best for clients is what makes Susan exceptional. What's more is her dedication to community and her thoughtful approach in the use of philanthropy in financial planning. This sets her apart and I would highly recommend her to anyone wishing to explore philanthropy as a strategic tool for personal wealth management.

Karen Young
President and CEO, Calgary United Way

A NEW WAY FORWARD
FOR WEALTH MANAGEMENT

A NEW WAY FORWARD

FOR WEALTH MANAGEMENT

Net Worth Thinking

SUSAN O'BRIEN

Copyright © 2019 by Susan O'Brien.

All rights reserved. No part of this book may be used or reproduced in any manner whatsoever without prior written consent of the author, except as provided by the United States of America copyright law.

Printed in the United States of America.

10 9 8 7 6 5 4 3 2 1

ISBN: 978-1-949639-39-1
LCCN: 2019910234

Cover and layout design by Wesley Strickland.

This publication is designed to provide accurate and authoritative information in regard to the subject matter covered. It is sold with the understanding that the publisher is not engaged in rendering legal, accounting, or other professional services. If legal advice or other expert assistance is required, the services of a competent professional person should be sought.

I would like to dedicate this book to my family, whose love and support sustains me, and to everyone who has placed their trust in me to help create and reach their goals.

I would also like to thank my writing coaches, Beth Herman and Elaine Best, my team at the Susan O'Brien Group, and everyone who has given me ideas and suggestions. Thank you, too, to everyone at Advantage for helping bring this book to life.

Contents

Introduction 1
MOST WEALTHY PEOPLE ARE ILL-SERVED

Chapter 1 11
THE CHECK-BOX CULTURE

Chapter 2 19
RETIREMENT PLANNING = FINANCIAL PLANNING LITE!

Chapter 3 27
MY STORY—AND HOW MY EXPERIENCE CAN BENEFIT YOU

Chapter 4 37
EVERY CUP OF COFFEE YOU BUY SAYS SOMETHING ABOUT YOU

Chapter 5 45
WHAT A REAL FINANCIAL PLAN LOOKS LIKE (START AT THE END, NOT AT THE BEGINNING)

Chapter 6 53
IT'S NOT JUST ABOUT YOUR WILL, IT'S ABOUT CREATING *GOOD* WILL

Chapter 7 .... *63*
FOMO: FEAR OF MISSING OUT!

Chapter 8 .... *73*
IF YOU DON'T PAY FOR A PLAN, IT'S WORTHLESS

Chapter 9 .... *83*
AN INVITATION TO CONTINUE THE CONVERSATION

Introduction

MOST WEALTHY PEOPLE ARE ILL-SERVED

It's a fallacy that the affluent are well served. Granted, they may be well served in some areas, but not when it comes to their money. High-net-worth individuals may have their choice of fabulous hotels, luxury spas, coveted seats at sporting events, and tables at five-star restaurants, but when it comes to making long-term decisions about their money, they're not getting the help they need. Most wealthy families do not have a financial plan in place—or if they do have one, it's sitting on a shelf, not getting updated every few months as it should be, and it's often never even executed to begin with.

Why is that?

You would think that money management should be a simple matter of dotting all the i's and crossing the t's, but the fact is, money can be a highly sensitive, emotionally fraught subject. One reason for this is family dynamics: Is a parent, sibling, or child estranged? Does someone in the family have a mental health issue? What about an overspending or a money management problem? When such complications intersect with potentially volatile issues such as succession planning, family wealth management becomes a complex puzzle.

At the very least, tackling the tough issues takes courage and commitment on the part of both the client and the financial advisor, who needs to know how to guide the conversation. Human beings tend to operate in pursuit or avoidance mode—that is, the pursuit of pleasure and the avoidance of pain—and sometimes people decide it's just easier not to broach the topic. Complacency feels a lot better in the short run. Unfortunately, there is a steep price to be paid for avoiding long-term planning.

WHY PEOPLE FAIL TO SEEK THE HELP THEY NEED

It can be frightening to open yourself up to a financial professional; you may feel exposed, like in one of those dreams in which you appear completely naked in public. But it needn't be like that. The right financial professional knows how to create an open, caring environment in which the client is made to feel safe. It is your advisor's job to help you determine how you will spend the rest of your life, and that means you need to be as open and frank as possible so that he or she can provide a comprehensive assessment of your situation. Telling only half the story, without bringing up the hard stuff, puts you both at a disadvantage.

Aside from the necessity of revealing delicate personal information, there is another reason many wealthy people are reluctant to seek professional guidance. To some, confessing a lack of knowledge in this area can be embarrassing—after all, C-suite executives and heads of family dynasties are supposed to have all the answers, right?

The truth is, no matter who we are and what station we've risen to in life, we can't know it all. The most successful people know when they don't know enough to keep the machine running, and they align themselves with people who have expertise in areas they don't.

The tendency not to seek expert help is encouraged by today's ubiquitous do-it-yourself attitude. Now, there's nothing wrong with taking a class or tutorial to learn a new subject or skill, but doing so doesn't make us instant experts! You can join a gym and lift some free weights, but taking the time to engage a personal trainer will help prevent injury and set you on a far more productive course to achieve your goals. Would you read a manual on dentistry and attempt to pull your own tooth? Of course you wouldn't. Designing and executing the best lifelong plan for your money is no different—it requires professional know-how.

A TAILORED, HOLISTIC APPROACH

Some people have negative feelings about the wealth management industry. We may regard financial advisors the same way we do lawyers; remember all those bad lawyer jokes? You may need them, but you fear they're going to take advantage of that need—and of your lack of expertise—by padding and overcharging. Though the financial services industry has been around for a long time, in some ways it's still in its infancy. For generations most people had pensions and didn't seek out financial professionals. Today people are living longer—and reaching the age of one hundred may be realistic. Consequently running out of money is a legitimate fear. Additionally there are fewer and fewer pensions, so most of us need professional wealth management advice.

Again, family wealth management is a complex business; laws and products are constantly evolving, and advisors must evolve as well to keep pace with those changes. But if they don't, it isn't always obvious? How will you know? An advisor may have a lot of different certifications, but it can be hard to figure out what they all mean and how they apply to your needs—if they do at all. You can tell whether someone has a degree from a good university, but is a certification worth anything?

One way to tell whether an advisor is competent and has your best interests at heart is to find out whether their wealth management advice is generally prescriptive or personally tailored to your specific needs. In recent years there has been a shift away from pure investment/asset management (products or commodity-like thinking) toward a much more holistic approach. This approach does not rely exclusively on stocks and bonds, nor does it focus on one-size-fits-all solutions such as prescribing mutual or exchange-traded funds. While there's nothing wrong with these products, today's top-of-the-line financial practitioners need to take into account many dozens of human variables.

When I first started out in the industry, I thought having my clients' best interests in mind meant picking out the best companies and products and putting together an investment portfolio. Things have changed considerably since then. If you meet with an advisor today and the first thing he or she tells you is to check out the performance of their stocks and bonds or what their best portfolios look like, that's the equivalent of seeing a doctor who reaches for the prescription pad without taking the time to give you a careful, individual diagnosis. What if your doctor automatically told you that you had cancer and that you'd need X number of chemotherapy treatments, without really understanding what kind of cancer you had or without even examining you and assessing your personal health history?

So many elements go into crafting the right portfolio for a client. Too many advisors simply say, "This is how we invest your money." But I have found it is best to work backward in a twelve-to-eighteen-month-long discovery process to figure out your individual needs and the amount of money you need to accumulate to live the life you desire.

Where are you today in relation to your goals? How do you want to live your life? How much risk can you afford to take? I want to know your concerns about estate planning, succession planning, and your children's and grandchildren's education. Who will take care of your children if something happens to you and your spouse? What about your animals? Many people consider them members of the family but don't think about what happens if there is no one around to care for them. Do you have family conflicts that could complicate either your legacy planning or succession planning for your business? All these bread-and-butter life issues and many more need to be considered in order to paint a complete financial picture.

> The right financial advisor will know what questions to ask to **HELP YOU ACHIEVE YOUR GOALS**

And what about personal desires—is there a special dream of yours that has long been subordinated to other, more "reasonable" goals? That may not have to be the case. How do you want to spend your days? What would your ideal life look like? The right financial advisor will know what questions to ask to help you achieve your goals. This individual will understand how to get to the heart of the matter in order to design the best of all possible long-term financial plans.

Many people who've been reluctant to engage a financial advisor in the past will wait until a crisis arises, expecting the advisor to make snap decisions and knee-jerk adjustments to a portfolio. I don't believe this scenario yields the best results, and any advisor worth his or her salt should take a comfortable amount of time to properly assess your needs. A responsible advisor makes careful recommendations rather than applying a Band-Aid that may come off in the next rainstorm.

THE OBSTACLES TO YOUR SUCCESS

Do you know what the biggest impediment to success is when it comes to managing your money? Contrary to what many people think, it's not fees. All too often it's investor behavior—in other words, your problem may be *you*.

As human beings, we want what we think everyone else is buying. We want what we're being told to buy on BNN. We want to get in before it's too late … and then we want to get *out* before it's too late. We're focused on the short term. Many investors make nothing because they rush to get in on a stock, buy more if it's rising—and then get rid of it the moment it starts to sink. And then the market crashes, fueling the rush to get out. Investors often are not in long enough to reap the rewards of a rebound. You need to stay invested in good and bad times, so a portfolio needs to be built to adjust and sustain itself in every possible market cycle.

I've also found that people often do not allow for inflation in their long-term financial plans. Some of them may have it somewhere in the back of their minds, but it needs to be at the forefront. Bit by bit, our purchasing power decreases over time. We know this intuitively because it costs more to buy groceries this year than it did last year. It costs more to travel. Your property taxes may have even doubled in the last year, as mine did. Over time it just costs more to live, and you need a portfolio that's going to outpace inflation—or it will whittle your money down to nothing.

You may be thinking of protecting your money by putting it in a "guaranteed" investment certificate or government bond. This is tantamount to saying you're willing to take a 2 percent pay cut each and every year (or 5 percent, depending on the rate of inflation), compounded over the next thirty years. It is not safe; in fact, there is actually a high risk that you will run out of money by doing this.

Another culprit eroding your purchasing power is taxes. Being tax efficient in your decisions and tax effective in your planning can mean the difference between running out of money, holding on to what you have, or growing it beyond your wildest imagination. Many CPAs are tax savvy on a personal and professional level—that is, they know how to save money on your individual and business income taxes—but their knowledge of you and your personal circumstances may not be deep or broad or integrated enough. We work very closely with your tax professionals to grow your money through integrated tax planning that fits your goals … something the right financial advisor should help you do.

SKIN IN THE GAME

It's common in the financial services industry for clients to pay for the investment product, such as the mutual fund in which they are investing, or perhaps to pay a fee for portfolio management. The rest of what needs to be done throughout the year—the financial advisor working with the client to update and reevaluate their portfolio based on changes in the business and the family—is basically done for free. These advisors perform hours and hours and hours of unbilled work for continuous financial planning over many years.

In the course of more than twenty years in this business (and a lifetime observing human nature), I've learned that when something is given away, the advisor may not be all that invested in it. Advisors need to feed their families, pay their bills, and maintain their lifestyles, just as you do—and unless you are volunteering your time for a worthy charity, you are not giving away your expertise and services.

In 2011 we came to the conclusion that we needed to charge a financial planning fee for our time and services. We also decided not to take on any clients without doing a comprehensive, integrated, "deep think" on their lives, as part of our vast plan for them. Since that time, we've found we are much better at our jobs because we are deeply invested. And we've discovered that our clients are better invested as well—they are much more open and honest about their lives, and more committed to getting us all the material we need. We are better equipped to do the best job we can right out of the starting gate, and everyone is fully committed to the outcome.

We are there to help you learn more about your financial life and to help you optimize it. In the chapters that follow, we will explore the best ways to build a robust life plan in order to achieve the very best you and your family can have.

Chapter 1

THE CHECK-BOX CULTURE

List-making is something most of us do. The idea has probably been around in one form or another for thousands of years, and to-do lists govern many people's daily lives. The practice of checking off completed tasks gives us a sense of accomplishment. Who doesn't want that?

There are people who live by lists. Billionaire Sir Richard Branson is known for his painstaking list-making. Very few of us enter a grocery store without a list of items to buy, and most of us make a list before tackling weekend chores. And what about Santa, who annually makes a list and checks it twice?

Sometimes lists are useful, but there are other times when ticking off boxes on a checklist fools us into thinking we've accomplished everything there is to accomplish. This is unproductive and can lead us down the wrong path.

In an effort to craft a financial plan, people often avail themselves of software designed to achieve that goal, sometimes on the advice of financial professionals. These applications ask basic questions about assets, liabilities, income, and expenses, and the clients move down the list, saying to themselves, "I've got this in place; I've got that in place; and that too. Check. Check. Check."

This accomplishes nothing. *Financial software is too narrowly designed and provides no room for context.* In short, it does not think. It's one size fits all—a check-box mentality—and that leads us to believe we've got it all handled when in fact we don't. Filling in the numbers after lunch on Saturday and then rushing off to the gym is no way to create a viable long-term financial plan.

A bona fide financial plan is more than a projection of future cash flow or how much money we can spend in retirement, contrary to what the software may lead us to believe. It involves in-depth conversations with a professional and careful analysis that gets to the root of your particular financial situation. Software can only do a fraction of that. It's important to examine all the tax, estate, insurance, and family matters that make up your finances. These pillars of your life are constantly evolving, and your financial plan needs to keep pace with that evolution.

As I said in the book's introduction, your financial situation is unique to you, and your advisor needs to treat it that way. Maybe one of your heirs is a spendthrift. Maybe someone has mental or physical disabilities that will require increasing levels of long-term care. There may be issues concerning legacy or philanthropy planning. All of these require fluency in a language that cold financial planning software just doesn't speak.

What about your will? How about the composition of your assets? If the will includes trusts but the ownership of assets precludes the actual funding of the trust, then the will fails. All of the planning and expense were for nothing. Perhaps in the next century, when artificial intelligence takes over the world, financial planning software will have a leg up on this (although I have my doubts), but it certainly doesn't today. For now, and for the foreseeable future, you need someone to take a holistic view and provide expert analysis and wise counsel so that you can formulate a plan, and then make sure the plan is actually executed. As in the above example with a failed will, failed planning is expensive.

Good intentions alone won't get your plan done—and if it doesn't get done, your return on your investments is ultimately a resounding zero.

SILOS: GOOD FOR GRAIN ... BUT NOT GOOD FOR YOUR MONEY

In the past, investing was all about products: An investment manager would come up with an investment plan for a portfolio, and you might have a different person to pick your stocks, plus a life insurance agent and a banker for your loans. An accountant would do your tax return, and a lawyer would draw up an estate plan. Everything was separate, or *siloed*, each area overseen by an individual with his or her own narrow area of expertise. There was no cohesive effort to map out the best long-term plan for your money because there was no one person pulling it all together.

This is actually quite common today in the medical profession, which is highly specialized. Chances are if we have five doctors with five specialties, each to help us with a different health issue, they do not communicate with one another. We can only hope that each doctor takes the time to peruse your list of medications in order to avoid prescribing something that will cause an undesirable interaction with something you're already taking—but unfortunately that's not always the case. Patients often end up in emergency rooms due to complications from drug interactions—an outcome that could have been avoided with better scrutiny and communication. The same is true about your money.

Sally and Bob first came to us when Bob was nearing retirement, in his midfifties. He'd spent his entire career in the oil and gas industry. Sally had supported Bob's career, which required him to put in long workdays, by staying home to raise their three children. When we met Bob and Sally, their children were attending university.

Bob's pension options were to choose a defined benefit contribution plan that would provide an income stream for life or to take the plan's commuted value and invest it. The deadline for the couple to make a decision was looming, and they came to us for help. We told them we couldn't help them without ascertaining their goals, their risk parameters, and what would be important to them for the rest of their lives. That analysis required us to examine all of their investment accounts; in the process, we learned they had twenty-five accounts spread across five financial institutions.

In each institution there is presumably an advisor doing a risk analysis and coming up with an investment mandate. So different people were looking at different pieces of Bob and Sally's puzzle without knowing what assets the couple had. Each had his or her own agenda, and each was seemingly unaware of the others. There was no confluence of planning among the five institutions, so the couple did not have an asset mix that really worked for them. We had trouble even determining what the income from the entire portfolio was in order to help them make the pension decision. Once we consolidated all those accounts into a single asset mix, we could more easily determine the risk in their portfolio and weigh the pros and cons of Bob's two available pension options.

We also learned in the process that Bob and Sally had a corporation, but they had not completely papered it; at that time only Bob was attached to it. We needed to incorporate Sally and their three adult children, and we did so. They could now have a capital gains exemption that allowed five people, instead of just one.

Digging down further, we examined the couple's wills and investments. As it turned out, the investments were not in Sally's name, but we realized that if we did a $2 million spousal loan from husband to wife, we could save them a substantial amount of income tax each and every year. Basically we were rearranging the asset structure—both within a corporate structure and individually—to save a significant amount of tax.

One of the delights in working with Sally and Bob was that they had immense gratitude for all they'd achieved in life and what they'd accumulated as a result. They wanted to give back to their community, so we set up a charitable foundation for them, a legacy that would live on for them through the generations.

No matter which pension option Bob and Sally chose, we soon determined they were never going to spend all their money. We decided to shelter some of it inside a life insurance policy that would be passed on to their children without anyone paying taxes on the proceeds.

The couple also believed that their three university-aged children might not make the same kind of income their father had earned in his profession, which would leave them unable to maintain the kind of lifestyle they'd grown up with. Sally and Bob wanted to help their children while they were alive, but they didn't want to simply hand them a big gift. At a family meeting, it was decided that the money would be given to the children in three separate tranches, rather than handing them a large chunk all at once that could be squandered on a foreign sports car or some such extravagance. The parents wanted to see exactly how each child would handle the money, so they would each get one tranche immediately, followed by another when each turned twenty-eight, and another when each turned thirty-two. The funds would be sufficient for a down payment on a house, or to spend on a wedding, or something else along those lines. Bob and Sally wanted to teach their children how to pace themselves and how to handle money.

* * *

The fact that Bob and Sally's assets were spread among five institutions is not all that unusual. People do this in the belief that they are somehow diversifying, perhaps thinking of the old adage about not putting all your eggs in one basket. Unfortunately, this behavior creates a highly complex situation. Diversification doesn't mean putting your assets in diverse institutions. Diversification means de-risking your portfolio through asset and security selection. You can have a wide variety of products and options, but it takes a single individual to pull it all together, to make a concerted effort to get to know you intimately, and to continually update the plan.

LOYAL TO A FAULT

The antithesis of Bob and Sally's story is the client who comes to us with a concentrated portfolio. Like Bob, Laurie spent her entire career—thirty years—in the energy industry. Laurie was the CEO of a major company, and all of her net worth was in company stock. But even if you are a CEO, you cannot control the economy. You cannot control the price of oil or gas. You cannot control the price of your company's stock. The only thing you *can* control is how you prepare for and react to unexpected events. With all of your eggs in this precarious basket, there is a tremendous risk of losing everything.

Laurie's loyalty ran deep. She professed that she was running the company and knew exactly what was going to happen. She came to us with a multimillion-dollar portfolio, wanting to set up a family trust to protect her assets from potential creditors. She would put just enough into the trust to take care of her husband's and her retirement income needs.

Among other things, we told her that, to accomplish this, we needed to sell off some of the company stock. She did not follow our recommendations, and today the value of her portfolio is down by half. As I said in the introduction, a big determinant in how you are going to emerge from your working years is investor behavior—*yours*.

Most people don't take into account how many moving pieces there are in a real financial plan. It's not only about software. It's not only about checking off boxes. It's not only about concentrating wealth or diversifying it. It's not only about assets, liabilities, income, and expenses. It's not only about family issues. It's not only about your values (which we will explore in depth in chapter 4). It's about all of the above … and much more!

In the next chapter, we'll talk about distinguishing between financial planning and retirement planning. Making money is very different from preserving money, and understanding the difference is vital to the health of your portfolio.

Chapter 2

RETIREMENT PLANNING = FINANCIAL PLANNING LITE!

Many people think retirement planning is equivalent to financial planning. People often use these terms interchangeably, but retirement planning is financial planning lite. It is not a fully realized, integrated, holistic financial plan.

The fact is that retirement planning is just one aspect of financial planning, just as flour is one component of a cake. You need many more ingredients to produce the desired result. A lot of financial planners will talk about a retirement plan as the whole picture, but it's not. A retirement plan is a cash flow projection. Period.

It takes a great deal of effort and planning and analysis to manage what you have, acquire what you need, and get from here to there in a long-term financial plan. Tax, estate, succession, philanthropy, insurance, *and* retirement planning are the tangible ingredients. Then there are the intangibles, such as personal values and legacy, which we will explore later in the book.

Many people fear that their lifestyle requirements, their generosity toward their children, and the increasing needs of their aging parents may cause them to run out of money—and with a simple retirement plan, as opposed to something more comprehensive, that just may happen.

So what can be done to ensure that you have all the money you need?

You must have a detailed, well-integrated blueprint for financial success. Your financial plan needs to start right here, right now, right where you are.

According to the Canadian Imperial Bank of Commerce (CIBC), nearly half—46 percent—of Canadians do not have any kind of plan in place.[1] In my own experience, only about 2 percent of clients who come to us have a plan. In part this is because people are focused more on the stock market and the performance of their portfolios than on the cohesiveness of their planning. Their big, burning question is what they should invest in. They come to us thinking they've missed out on something or that they're not investing properly, or they want to know why someone else is getting a great return on their investments but they are not. They may have an accountant doing their taxes, and perhaps a lawyer drew up their will, but as I explained in chapter 1, nobody's integrated everything ... or anything! Their funds are siloed: there simply is no plan.

---

1   "Nearly Half of Canadians Lack a Financial Plan, Putting Their Goals at Risk," Canadian Imperial Bank of Commerce, January 24, 2017, accessed May 1, 2018, http://cibc.mediaroom.com/2017-01-24-Nearly-half-of-Canadians-lack-a-financial-plan-putting-their-goals-at-risk-CIBC-Poll.

TIMES CHANGE, AND YOU NEED TO CHANGE WITH THEM

The few who do have a plan have typically done nothing with it. In my twenty years as a financial professional, I can recall only one client who came to us with a comprehensive, *fully executed* financial plan for himself and his family. He came to us with a need for investment management but ended up with much more. We reviewed the existing plan and decided that it was solid, but it needed updating, because financial plans are dynamic. There had been changes in these people's lives, as there are in everyone's—children enter university or graduate, a grandchild is born, parents begin to age, tax situations change because someone may not be working—and going forward we would need to begin monitoring for more changes. Change can affect the present as much as the future. It all needs to be addressed on an ongoing basis.

GO FROM BAD TO DIVERSE

A comprehensive, un-siloed plan also requires you to diversify. As I said in chapter 1, many people invest in what they believe they can control. They may have very concentrated stock positions in the companies for which they work, but they cannot control the economy or the stock market. **Not diversifying out of that position—maybe out of a misplaced sense of loyalty—is a formula for failure.** You may be somewhat reluctant to diversify from company stock if you're a major executive in your company, but it is absolutely crucial to do so. Of course you need to be strategic about selling it, but it has to be done or your retirement can be jeopardized.

GENEROUS TO A FAULT?

It is dangerous to have a simple retirement plan that zeroes in on cash flow to the exclusion of other considerations: Other factors can derail the plan if they are not taken into account. One example is the generosity factor.

Ellen, a widow in her midsixties, was living off the royalties from a software patent her late husband had created. She had a considerable amount of money—but she also had two children in their forties to whom she'd been gifting a lot of that money. She'd built houses for each of them, and they were both living in them rent-free. She paid the property taxes, utilities, and homeowners insurance, and she was picking up the tab for each grandchild's education.

When we first sat down with Ellen, we expected her to have considerable concerns about running out of money. In fact, her concerns were of a different nature: she was afraid she was not treating her two adult children equally, worried that one had gotten a bigger house than other, and so on.

When we created her financial plan, we were frank. We explained to her that if she continued in the direction she was headed, she was going to run out of money. "You could live another twenty years or more," I told her, "and you could end up having to spend six months of the year living at one child's home, then the other."

At that point, because of her generosity and the fact that her adult children had become habituated to her largesse, she could not afford to fix the roof on her own house or install a new furnace—and let's face it, Canada is *cold*. At one point Ellen even considered selling her home to keep her children in the lifestyle they were accustomed to, with the rationale that she didn't need such a big place herself. When we explained to her that she didn't have to give up her entire life, as she was in the process of doing, she ultimately admitted she loved the view and would hate to leave. *Leave?* How unfortunate that this had even been a consideration for her.

At a family meeting, with Ellen's permission, we explained to her children that their mother would not be able to continue doing all she was doing for them. While one of the siblings was not happy—in fact, he exhibited a response that bordered on rage—the other one readily accepted the circumstances.

Family meetings are often challenging, but preserving your money requires that you step back and become equal to the task. I give a lot to my children and the philanthropic causes I believe in, but we all need to give within the means that we have. Sometimes we can be generous to a fault.

IT ALL ADDS UP

When we create a financial plan for the rest of your life, it's important that we have all the documents necessary for a proper review. These include any plans you may have in place, financial statements from institutions where you may be investing, tax returns, any tax planning that was done previously, information about charitable foundations that may be set up, family trusts, wills, powers of attorney, personal directives, employee benefits, benefits outside of work, work pension plans, insurance documents, and government plans such as old-age security and Canada pension plans. We also need to know about your financial responsibilities and obligations—children, parents, and anything else.

THE NEXT GENERATION

A complete financial plan also needs to take into account the importance of properly setting your children up to receive their inheritance. This means teaching them to manage money. Sometimes we may put language in a will specifying that children will get money at various stages, and that they need to meet with attorneys and us as their financial professionals to make sure the succession plan is being executed properly. We are there in the setup of the plan and we know the planning and rationale for the decisions; so we are best able to make sure the planning is implemented.

Children need to learn budgeting and saving at as early an age as possible. It's important for us to be able to impress upon the next generation that the longer they wait to take these steps, the more compromised their lives will be. Getting into the habit of saving 10 percent or even 5 percent of your paycheck can make you wealthy later in life if you plan carefully, but most people just don't do it.

We're in it for the long haul. When members of the next generation get a first job, we help them choose the right savings, benefits, and retirement plans. Our efforts to make them financially savvy begin as early as possible and are ongoing. There's an old expression, "shirtsleeves to shirtsleeves in three generations." It means that one generation makes a fortune by dint of hard work and careful investment. They are prudent and thrifty because they generally started with nothing and built something of value. The next generation lives a much more extravagant lifestyle, flying first class, seeing the world, and spending the hard-earned money of the first generation. By the third generation, there is no money left. They are once again starting with nothing. If we can prevent shirtsleeves to shirtsleeves in three generations from happening, we've done our jobs.

Chapter 3

MY STORY—AND HOW MY EXPERIENCE CAN BENEFIT YOU

Some people live for numbers. Math is their *métier*. For them it's better than Godiva chocolate or that third cup of espresso. We've all seen them portrayed on TV and in the movies wearing nerdy glasses and plastic pocket protectors. While I don't tend to accessorize that way, math has always been my forte, and besides coming easily to me … okay, *I really do love it!*

In fact I'm passionate about many things. Curious and doggedly inquisitive while growing up, I wanted to experience the world in every possible way. This meant I wanted a CCM ten-speed bike I could use to explore the neighborhood and a pair of state-of-the-art running shoes in which to go as fast and far as I could. But in my family, if you really wanted something, you had to go to work for it.

From the time I was fourteen, I was volunteering in a senior citizens' home; when they found out I was legally too young, I had to go. Loving work, I soon found a paid summer job. I worked hard, and with a few choice exceptions like the bike, athletic shoes, and even a trip with friends to Hawaii when I was seventeen (yes, I was enough of a saver to pay for the trip myself), I saved most of my money. In fact, I became a kind of family banker for my older sister and younger brother. Unfortunately, it would be a long time before I learned that I should have been charging interest!

In high school I had two big passions: history (an interest that may have had something to do with my crush on the teacher) and economics. Can you guess which one ultimately won out? The big career decision didn't happen until I attended the University of Toronto, though, when a counselor noticed my strong aptitude for mathematics and steered me toward finance. The decision was a good one—and besides, by then I'd discovered that history involved too much writing, and I could not type. It was a time before personal computers, and the fact that I didn't have to labor over a typewriter pecking out long historical essays letter by letter was a real incentive for a life in numbers.

I inhaled all the curves in economics; I thought the supply and demand curves were beautiful. I thought, "This is so easy! Give me more!" You just move around the curves and get the answers, plain and simple. Most things in life are not black and white, but this subject was—there was only one answer to any given problem. I used to tutor my roommate, wondering why she—or everyone, for that matter—didn't understand and *love* this subject matter.

With finance and economics clearly in my DNA, and armed with a bachelor of commerce degree, I went to work as a tax interpretations officer for the Canada Revenue Agency right out of university in 1982. My job was to master tax law, specifically in regard to commodity tax, and then interpret it when people called or wrote in with questions.

I loved tax law (here come the nerd glasses). I reveled in reading everything I could about tax legislation to figure out how it could be applicable to businesses. I even thought about becoming a tax lawyer, as I knew I could do some real good in that profession by saving clients money that they could then invest elsewhere. But that sort of work didn't feel as personal as I'd have liked. If I'd gone to work in that realm, I'd have been dealing with big companies—not individuals. There was nothing really *human* about it.

While I found working for the government to be a bit confining, it was nonetheless rewarding. The following year, believing that private industry offered more opportunity, I parlayed my experience into a job as a tax manager for Union Carbide. Eventually I moved on to another company, TaxSave Consultants, where my job was to review the taxes our client companies were paying and identify where they might have missed out on tax opportunities. I would then approach the Canada Revenue Agency (my old stomping grounds) on the client's behalf. If you know tax law inside out, you can negotiate quite successfully on behalf of these businesses and save them vast amounts of money.

In 1989 I went to work for Deloitte Chartered Accountants as a senior tax manager, looking to expand my knowledge base and broaden my skill set. When I was sure I'd accumulated a vast store of knowledge, I began to have a gnawing feeling that it was time to go to work for myself.

THE LEAP

At thirty-three, I was now thinking hard about what I really wanted my life to look like. Many entrepreneurs seem to start their own ventures around that time of life, and I guess I was no different. I was ready to strike out on my own and sink or swim under my own banner. It was time to do something for myself—something that ignited my passion and used all of my skills.

So I started Susan O'Brien and Associates—my own tax-consulting firm. I had accumulated knowledge from my days at the CRA in a corporate environment and in a major chartered accounting firm, and I was ready. The first time I called a potential client, though, I almost lost my voice and my knees buckled.

My philosophy was that I could not fail and that I could start my own successful business.

While that was the goal, the hard fact was that I was going to have to start all over again, taking a huge earnings cut, as many do when we start down our own road. I'd been doing very well financially and was the main support for our growing family. Needless to say, Susan O'Brien and Associates was even more successful than I thought, earning $500,000 dollars in revenue in its first year of operation.

But as the saying goes, it's not all about the money. This was a transaction-based business and I wanted more. I wanted to acquire my own special clients and get to know each one on an individual basis. My philosophy was—and is—that if I know what's important to you, your business, and your family, I can do much more to make your financial dreams become a reality for you. I don't run a one-size-fits-all kind of operation. I wanted to make a real difference in people's lives. I was walking around with a hollow feeling. I wanted to challenge myself to do more, not only for myself but for the people I served. I worked unrelentingly hard at that.

Five years later, in 1998, I started a new venture, the Susan O'Brien Group, with a large global Canadian bank, where I am today. I'd learned my tax-consulting craft and had opened many doors for myself, ultimately finding that my heart was in wealth management.

While I knew a lot of people, in order to build this business, a small boutique within a large firm, I had to start over almost from scratch … again. I literally opened the phone book and started calling people with whom I wanted to do business, whether I knew them or not, asking if they wanted a second opinion on their investments. We used to call it dialing for dollars, and the process worked for introductions. Just like that scene in the movie *The Wolf of Wall Street*, in which Leonardo DiCaprio calls people to say he has a great investment idea for them. He didn't have one, I did.

It was a fairly common practice twenty years ago, and in those days, financial management was mostly picking the right stocks for people. I must admit I loved the sizzle of the stock market, and I still do, but wealth management is much more than that.

Just before I started the Susan O'Brien Group, I went to the bank and took out a big line of credit to keep my family in the same house. I was still the chief breadwinner, now in a family with four young children, and I didn't want to sell our home—to have the people I loved the most pay the price to advance my aspirations.

I didn't have much of an income, if any, for a long time, and it was five years before I could call myself a viable and sustainable business. I've always said that many people are afraid of success and do things to sabotage themselves (or maybe they just lack the patience and persistence to sit on the phone long enough to drum up the business they need). I, on the other hand, was afraid of failure.

I have always cautioned my clients very strongly not to jeopardize their retirement, but that is exactly what I did. I also perpetually robbed Peter to pay Paul. It was frightening and frustrating, and anyone who hasn't been in that position cannot fathom what it feels like to go home each night pretty much empty-handed—and empty-hearted as a result. I felt as though I were letting everyone down. It was a very challenging time, to say the least.

At one point, after having been entirely self-sufficient for years and years, I had to ask my parents whether I could borrow money; for someone like me, this was worse than cold calling! It wasn't that they weren't loving and caring parents, nor was it that they couldn't afford to help me out; they certainly could. But the act of asking for help felt like an admission of inadequacy. I had children, a mortgage, and other responsibilities, however, and I knew I would not fail. I took a good, hard look at my life and faced my weak spots, and that self-examination gave me a powerful foundation from which to counsel clients.

STARVING AND STAYING

It takes a long time for anyone to become established in the financial field. You need time to build your business, even if you're under the auspices of a larger institution as I was, and there generally isn't any kind of playbook. In the days when I was getting my sea legs, an institution might hire you, but unscrupulous managers or colleagues, and let's face it, every industry has a few, often wanted you to fail so they could take your clients. You might fight your way through the hard work of starting from scratch and collect a few clients, but those few might not be enough for you to survive, and you'd starve yourself out of the business.

Nevertheless, I stuck it out—again, because I wanted to make a significant difference in people's lives. Today my company is a seventeen-time award-winning wealth advisory practice geared to high-net-worth individuals. *That's* why I stuck to my guns even when the going was hard.

Soon after I started the Susan O'Brien Group, I had the opportunity to work with Henry and Dina, a married couple in their early seventies. Henry and Dina had recently retired when they came to me, and like many people in their situation, they were deeply concerned that they wouldn't have enough money to last to the end of their lives. To complicate matters further, their adult children lived out of town and therefore would not be able to help when Henry and Dina's physical needs inevitably began to increase as they got older. I dug deep in our conversations and learned that they'd never, until that moment, received financial advice of any kind—except to keep doing what they were doing—when their overwhelming fears of running out of money brought them to me.

Children of the Great Depression, all Henry and Dina knew was to hold tight to their money, which they did in the form of guaranteed investment certificates—little more than a glorified savings account. When I asked them what they wanted, they confessed that they really didn't know. They had no idea what to do with their money. And their fears were well founded: had they left all their money in GICs, they would have completely run out.

In the course of the next twenty years, I worked regularly with Henry and Dina on their portfolio, and in time they were able to afford to move into a senior living home. Henry recently passed away, but he and Dina never did run out of money. They had a good life in retirement and told me often that their friends were losing sleep trying to figure out how to make their own money last. But for Dina and Henry, it became a non issue.

KNOWLEDGE QUEST: ABI!

There's a motto I live by: Always Be Improving, or in today's acronym-obsessed world, ABI. It may sound like a cliché, but no one gets anywhere in life without constant self-improvement. In my role as a financial professional, I'm in an evolving industry: The laws, products, and people are always changing. If I don't change and evolve to keep pace with it all, I am of no use to my valued clients who trust me. I also need to continually move my comfort zone. You do that when you are in an ABI mode.

I am truly inspired by my clients, and I want to do my best for them every single day. Continuing education and constant reading enables me to do that. I have to stay ahead of the curve; otherwise, how can I provide useful advice? I usually spend the first couple of hours of my day reading: What's new with the Ontario budget, or the Alberta budget? What's new in the tax legislation arena? What's new with RSP contribution limits? What about the stock market and the economy in general? Pension legislation? What about changes to American law? We frequently encounter cross-border issues because we often work with American executives who reside in Canada.

A financial professional needs to listen to clients to figure out what they really need and the best way to provide it for them. Henry Ford famously said that if he'd asked his customers what they wanted, they'd have told him, "a faster horse." But he had a better idea. I am vitally interested in what my clients want and need, but it is also incumbent upon me to deliver it in the best possible way—and sometimes that means finding ways they might not have thought of on their own. That's why I work in financial services. Pocket protector notwithstanding, I can't think of a better life.

Chapter 4

EVERY CUP OF COFFEE YOU BUY SAYS SOMETHING ABOUT YOU

Sarah has goals and expenses like the rest of us. She wants to take care of her family and her retirement in the best way possible. Among her expenses is a coffeehouse tab of $1,400 a year. Sarah's husband, Richard, spends around the same amount, so together the couple spends around $2,800 a year on coffeehouse drinks. Sure, we all want our coffee, and there's something to be said for the way a rich, steamy latte girds us for our morning. But there is also something to be said for investing that money elsewhere—for instance, in a child's education fund.

As high as that figure seems just for coffee, it's reasonable to assume you spend it if you stop for coffee each day on your way to work. I've heard it said that *Shark Tank*'s infamous "Mr. Wonderful," Kevin O'Leary, avoids those establishments, preferring to spend a mere eighteen cents a day on his morning java, presumably at home or at the office. He then prudently invests the difference.

So what does that say about the way *you* do things?

It's likely your habits fall somewhere in between Sarah and Richard's and Kevin O'Leary's. Pleasure and enjoyment are necessary in life, and my intention is not to single out coffeehouses as the root of all evil. But clearly O'Leary has taken a step back to think about what's most important to him, and his values are reflected in his spending habits. Unfortunately, most people lead unexamined lives in this respect. They haven't pondered what's really important to them ... what their values are. When was the last time you spent more than a couple of minutes *really* thinking about what matters most in your own plan for the rest of your life?

> Values are important because they support a life of authenticity, **IN WHICH ACTIONS AND VALUES ARE ALIGNED**

Values are important because they support a life of authenticity, in which actions and values are aligned. Today many of us don't live in accordance with our values. Our actions are dictated by our desire to keep up with neighbors, coworkers, friends, relatives—even someone we may have passed on the street who *appeared* to have it all. We allow ourselves to be seduced into carrying around that daily venti hazelnut mocha coconut milk macchiato, buying a Prada bag or a catamaran, or maintaining a star architect–designed coastal home that we enjoy just a few times a year. You do things because you think that's the way you *should* live. After all, you work exceedingly hard and you deserve it! But you don't step back and ask yourself if that's really the life you need to be living—or that you even *want* to be living. Ask yourself whether your life is one that feels right to you, not someone else's life or dream, and not their expectation of how yours should look.

There are times in my own life when I am compelled to reexamine what's really important to me. I need to reflect on how I am spending my money. Has anything changed since I considered my lifestyle and money situation five years ago, or even two years ago? Have there been any new developments? Are there any new challenges or goals? What makes me feel truly happy?

LINING UP

That gnawing feeling of discontent clients sometimes express to me often comes from lives that do not align with what's intrinsically important to them. They are living outside their value system—not living authentically. I always ask if they are spending their wealth in a way that's affording them satisfaction. It can be hard to answer these kinds of questions, and sometimes the answers are not readily apparent, but challenging yourself to dig deep and think about your values more often than not yields huge dividends. We live in a fast-paced, dynamic world—the check-box culture we talked about in chapter 1—and we feel driven to check off boxes on to-do lists, moving as quickly as possible on to the next task. But what about *thinking* about the tasks you perform, as opposed to racing them to the finish line? What about digging deep and seeing exactly the kind of life you want for yourself today?

Many of us go through life without really thinking. We put ourselves on automatic pilot, and we focus on spending and acquiring, and more spending and acquiring. But what is the real purpose of the money you are working so hard to accumulate? Reviewing how you currently spend your money and then analyzing it may reveal you are not spending it in accordance with your values. Going through this planning myself helped me to figure out that I could be more generous in my gifts to charity.

A NEW WAY FORWARD FOR WEALTH MANAGEMENT

* * *

Kathryn and David, a nurse and a dentist married for more than twenty years, are both high-income individuals. They came to my firm in their midforties, having made a great deal of money. The problem was that they had overspent in trying to maintain a certain lifestyle, and they were afraid they would run out of money. They owned a very expensive home and had a second property. They liked a lot of toys (bikes, cars, and electronics) and loved to travel. They had a very young child for whose education they needed to save. They were living the kind of lifestyle they thought they should be living, just kind of going along each day without analyzing what they were doing. They agreed to submit to our twelve-to-eighteen-month discovery process, allowing us to have important conversations with them to uncover their true values.

It soon became clear that Kathryn and David had to change the way they lived or they were going to run out of money.

Changing one's lifestyle is one of the hardest things to do. If you're living a certain way, you don't want to be told you need to cut back. While we never lecture a client, it's hard for people to hear about whether they need to reconsider their spending habits, and/or whether they're prepared for an illness or injury that could derail them for a long period of time (or permanently).

In time we were able to make Kathryn and David understand that while they didn't have to downsize their primary home or get rid of their toys, they needed to sell their second property. We came to this conclusion by asking how much it cost to maintain, how often they used it, and how much enjoyment they got from it—that is, how important it really was to them overall. Investing the money they would make from the sale of the property would have a significant impact on the rest of their lives, so there really was no question about the right thing to do. They came to understand that the longer they waited to sell, the more likely it was that the sale would come too late for them to accumulate all they needed in order not to run out of money. A portfolio needs time to grow, and if they elected to sell right away, they'd have at least ten years (their targeted retirement time) before they'd need to live off the portfolio, and the sale of the second home would make that a comfortable reality.

I often use the following example that I learned years ago from a leader in the financial services field of someone going to the doctor and asking for sleeping pills because they can't sleep. The doctor says, "Actually, you don't need sleeping pills. You weigh three hundred pounds, you have high cholesterol, diabetes, and you are stressed out all the time. You need to make lifestyle changes."

In the same way, someone will come to me saying she needs a bigger return on her investments. "I just need to make more money, and if I make more money right now, everything will be fine." But just like those sleeping pills, making more money right now, even if possible, is likely a temporary fix that treats the symptoms and not the disease. Without a lifestyle reevaluation, more money right now may translate into investing in speculative securities—which may serve as a Band-Aid but can actually result in losing more money in the long run. And chances are the more money this individual makes, the more she will spend, because there is no lifestyle adjustment. Something's gotta give.

Determining the "whys" of overspending is the key to a more sustainable lifestyle. It's not just about getting better performance from your assets; it's about taking a good, hard look at your life. How do you want to live today so you're not always borrowing at the end of every year to maintain your lifestyle?

ABOVE THE LAW (OF WISE CHOICES)

A prospective client came into our office in a desperate situation. He was a lawyer who made a million dollars a year. But each year he got into more and more debt. As hard as I tried to get at the crux of the matter—why he chose to perpetuate this unsustainable lifestyle that increased his stress level—I simply could not. He knew it was wrong, but he and his wife were just unwilling not to fly out to a second property on weekends. They were unwilling to make any changes in their lifestyle whatsoever. I even explained that at a minimum he needed to carry some life insurance, as he had three children and a spouse who didn't work. If nothing else, he needed to protect his family. But I could not get him to move on any recommendations whatsoever. He thought he'd just work forever, even though he was overly stressed and anxious every time we met in person or spoke on the phone, and I knew that was a recipe for disaster. He was getting older, and inevitably his health would catch up with him.

Statistics show that 60 percent of people do not choose their retirement date. They may start out intending to, but life takes over. They may find themselves caregivers to aging parents or a spouse who is ill. They may get laid off or become injured or ill themselves. The long, financially stable career and good health we expect for ourselves often doesn't happen. Life happens instead. So we need to have conversations long before this in order to decide who and what are really important in our lives.

CAUGHT IN THE ACT (OF GIVING)

Believe it or not, overspending can also manifest itself in the virtue of generosity. Most of us want to give, but do we know when *what* we give and *how* we give are just too much?

Giving can be a sensitive, emotionally charged subject when family members or friends prevail upon us for help, and certainly charities and other philanthropic pursuits will always come calling, tugging at our heartstrings. Maybe a family member has experienced a serious illness, and we may want to go to the ends of the earth to help fund research and find a cure. But is it possible to go too far? While strategic philanthropy is something I endorse, as it benefits both the recipient and the giver, some people overspend in their efforts to help. It's important to discover what is at the heart of your giving—why, where, and how often you do it—and structure the way in which you give.

Once again, your personal values come into play here because they will determine the course you take. Maybe taking a step back from that venti caramel macchiato to see how and why you do things says something very important about you.

Chapter 5

WHAT A REAL FINANCIAL PLAN LOOKS LIKE (START AT THE END, NOT AT THE BEGINNING)

Financial portfolios are quite often a composite of stocks, bonds, and mutual funds that an advisor or multiple advisors may have suggested. The result looks like a solid investment management portfolio, but what is it *really*?

What it's *not* is something tailored to you as an individual. I've said it before and I cannot say it enough: *There is nothing individual or personal in a portfolio of this nature.* It's not going to anticipate your family's evolving needs, nor will it take into account your values and legacy. The desire for growth may have been there when you invested in stock X and mutual fund Y, but how will that growth be channeled to protect you and your family—and in what ways, and for how long? A one-size-fits-all portfolio offers no guarantee that you will not run out of money.

While a portfolio filled with stocks, bonds, and mutual funds may look like just the ticket at first, it is often the result of the check-box mentality we talked about in chapter 1. In time, when people start to think more about what they have and don't have, and certainly what they will need, the idea of running out of money begins to keep them up at night. They may go back to their advisor to devise some kind of plan, but that doesn't work: Very often advisors who primarily choose stocks, bonds, and/or mutual funds are not qualified to do comprehensive financial planning, and they're the first to tell you that their expertise is limited to investment management. What's more, creating a financial plan on top of a portfolio that's already in place may only force the proverbial square pegs into round holes. Maybe the components of your portfolio are going to work as parts of a plan to ensure your future and maybe they aren't, but odds are a portfolio built on what's hot at the moment is going to fail in the long run because it has nothing to do with your long-term needs.

At the outset of a meeting with a new client, the first thing I do is start at the end—not the beginning. While that may sound confusing, the fact is I want to know your personal story before I look at anything in which you may have already invested; your existing portfolio gets put on the back burner. So essentially I'm coming in at the end of your investment history, presumably after you've been accumulating what you have for years—and setting it all aside. I want to determine what your goals are for yourself, your family, your retirement, and more—everything we've discussed in the previous chapters. We cannot build an investment portfolio for you until we take a deep dive into your life. Only after we've done that will we evaluate your existing investments to determine whether what you have even correlates with what you've told us.

TAKE TWO (OR MORE) PIECES OF ADVICE AND CALL US IN THE MORNING

It's only when we've got the right diagnosis that we can write the proper prescription. Bill and Audra came to us in their late forties when Bill had been laid off after twenty-five years at the same company. Audra had previously been employed as an obstetrical nurse, but had taken the past few years off going back to school and looking at new opportunities. Though now she was reconsidering the idea of trying to find another job at her age and found it was not all that appealing. Understandably, Bill's biggest concern was whether any employer would hire him at his age and whether he would be at the same salary level if anyone did hire him. Though age discrimination is illegal, the reality is that many people in their fifties and sixties find it difficult to compete with younger workers because employers may feel they are nearing retirement age. In Bill's case, further investigation on our part revealed that he really didn't want to go back to work because, as he put it, he was pretty burned out.

They brought in their investment portfolio and asked whether they had enough money to live off for the rest of their lives. Bill was also trying to choose one of the pension options presented to him—before the company deadline—and couldn't decide which was best. The couple was anxious and tried to hurry us along, but we explained to them that we needed time to do some discovery—to discuss their values, needs, and goals—in order to help them make sustainable choices. In this case the issue was compounded by the fact that we didn't trust the long-term ability of this particular company to honor its pension obligations to Bill, so we had to be very careful.

Here, again, it was about a lot more than evaluating an investment portfolio and choosing a pension plan. Once we found out that their ideal lifestyle in retirement involved world travel—not just a week-long cruise now and then, but spending months in various locales to immerse themselves in the culture—we had to figure out how that could work. They had dreamed about spending three months in Italy and perhaps the next three months in Vietnam, and so on.

Where the pension was concerned, we decided that taking the commuted value would be a safer way to go. We did a break-even analysis between leaving the money with the company and taking the money outright, considering what rate of return he'd need from his portfolio. At that point we'd still not constructed the new portfolio, but factoring in the rate of return from the pension funds and anything else we were considering, vis-à-vis retirement ideas, set us on the right course.

Bill's s existing holdings indicated he was 100 percent invested in Canada, and 20 percent of his Canadian holdings were in company stock. It was both too risky and too concentrated. There was nowhere near enough diversification to protect the couple in a capricious economic climate. First, we recommended he eliminate all of his company stock exposure by selling those shares. We then came up with a portfolio suited to their retirement income needs and which also met their risk parameters. It was a portfolio designed to minimize risk. Our investment plan for Bill and Audra was designed for them never to have to work again and to provide sufficient income so that they would never run out of money.

Once we assessed their lives in retirement and stepped back to analyze their initial portfolio, we learned they were carrying disability insurance. We canceled that because there's no sense paying into a disability policy—which is income replacement—if you are not working. Critical illness coverage was continued, as it has nothing to do with job income.

There were other issues we needed to correct in the existing plan. We recommended they keep their life insurance. But when we looked at their estate planning documents, and in particular at their wills, we found a problem: Most couples leave everything to each other, but this was a second relationship for Bill and Audra and they had not done that. Bill had left only part of his assets to Audra, and she'd left all of her assets to Bill. The rest went to family members and charity. We questioned the rationale behind these actions. What if Bill died first and Audra had only part of the assets? Would she run out of money? What if she died first? Would Bill be all right? How do extended family members and charity fit into the goals of the couple? Are they as important as when the couple set up their wills fifteen years ago? How would all of this change our recommendations for Bill and Audra?

A real financial plan takes into account all kinds of family issues and goals. Had we simply reviewed Bill and Audra's investment portfolio when they walked through the door and said, "This one is a good investment and that one is not," they would have been ill served. We had to know their story first.

MAKING LIFESTYLE CHANGES

Mia is a successful construction industry executive in her fifties. When she came to us, her portfolio contained a multitude of real estate properties; in fact, 80 percent of it was in real estate, both for her own use—in the form of three homes—and as rental properties concentrated in one geographic area. She was like so many people who feel comfortable investing in what they know—often to their detriment. The remainder of the portfolio comprised investments in

Canadian companies. She had two grown children whose education she'd already paid for, and she was looking to retire within about five years.

Pro forma, we immediately set that aside to ascertain what her real goals were, including how much money she needed in retirement. We talked about tax and estate planning, tax saving, and insurance, and asked the all-important question: What if she couldn't work (i.e., did she have disability insurance?), or if she didn't survive the next five years (her children were important to her and she wanted to create an estate for them; i.e., did she have life insurance so her adult children would have something when she was gone?)?

When the discovery was over, then and only then did we take a significant look at her assets, whereupon we learned Mia's portfolio wouldn't actually generate enough income for her to reach and maintain her retirement goals. She would need to make some lifestyle changes—which is the hardest thing for most people to do. It's not always easy for us to show people the consequences of their decisions, but we had to explain to Mia that if she kept on the way she was going, she would jeopardize the kind of retirement she was anticipating—a retirement she wanted sooner rather than later.

In this case, we recommended she strategically sell off some of her rental real estate because it was not generating enough income to offset the cost of all the maintenance and repairs. Add to that the fact that all of her investments were in Canada, and the Canadian market had been doing terribly. Mia's faith in investing was low because she hadn't seen much, if anything, in the way of returns.

When we met with her again, we explained that her investment portfolio was not designed as a retirement portfolio. Among other things, it was not properly allocated and diversified. We would have to introduce US and global companies. We'd have to bring in fixed income components, bonds, preferred stock, and alternative investments. Her portfolio needed to start generating retirement income, and of course she'd have to make some hard decisions about her personal real estate. Alternatively, Mia could decide to work longer and save more to put toward her retirement income.

These kinds of conversations are crucial when deciding how the rest of your life is going to look—and again, had we studied her portfolio first without asking about her real goals, we might have simply made suggestions and recommendations about what she already had. Unfortunately, Mia chose not to take any action whatsoever and ultimately did not become a client.

However, a surgeon and her stay-at-home husband we represented did take action, and it made all the difference in the quality of their lives.

Sharon and David were in their late forties with a young son still at home when we first met them. After we'd taken the time to sit down with the couple and outline their values, legacy ideas, and retirement goals, and only when we'd finished all that did we examine their portfolio and recommend selling some of their real estate that we viewed as problematic. It took a while—actually four to five years—to sell all of it, but they were better off for having divested themselves of these lifestyle properties, which were just too large a piece of their portfolio to support their ideal lifestyle in retirement. They heeded our real estate advice, along with some other recommendations (like Bill and Audra, they were insufficiently diversified, with heavy emphasis on Canada), and were able to achieve a great deal of peace, knowing they no longer had to worry about how they'd spend the rest of their lives. They now had the peace of mind they would never run out of money and were financially confident.

Chapter 6

IT'S NOT JUST ABOUT YOUR WILL, IT'S ABOUT CREATING *GOOD* WILL

Let's face it: more often than not, family dynamics are a chaotic stew. Many best-selling books have been written and Academy Award–winning movies have been made on the subject, and there is no shortage of material. And when money is introduced into the mix, it can open up the floodgates, resulting in all kinds of bad behavior. According to a 2014 Wealth-X and NFP Family Wealth Transfers Report, $16 trillion dollars of ultra-high-net-worth wealth, or UHNW, is expected to be transferred to the next generation over the next thirty years.[2] This can present major communication challenges for any family with significant assets that must be distributed.

The explosive *Leon v. Leon* case is a perfect example of such a situation. Terry Leon, CEO of Leon's Furniture Ltd., is being sued by Anita Leon, the widow of his deceased brother, Tom. Anita claims that Terry, in collusion with Tom's other brothers, Robert and Kevin,

---

2   Wealth-X and NFP Family Wealth Transfers Report 2014, 5, http://www.wealthx.com/wp-content/uploads/2015/01/WealthX_NFP_FamilyWealth-TransfersReport-2014.pdf.

is withholding money from a Leon family trust that was intended to benefit her and her late husband.

The problem arose from the byzantine nature of the family's finances. In order to defer capital gains taxes and maintain the family's control over their business, trust investments were set up in 1998 that included voting shares in Leon's Furniture. All of the Leon children were put in direct control of their own trusts—except for Tom, whose longtime US residency posed a problem. Because the Leon family and their company are Canadian, Tom's direct ownership of shares in the Leon company would have had, as the *Calgary Herald* put it, "significant cross-border tax implications."[3] So Terry, Robert, and Kevin were appointed trustees of a trust whose beneficiaries were Tom and Anita—and because Tom and Anita had no children of their own, the children of Tom's siblings were named as secondary beneficiaries. When Tom became seriously ill in 2012 and asked for additional money from the trust to help with medical expenses, his brothers looked into his finances and discovered that he had considerable debt, and they refused to release the funds.

Tom died in 2016, and as of this writing, the matter remains unresolved (it was expected to go to trial in December 2018). Terry's sister Marjorie has taken Anita's side, and intra-family relationships appear to have been permanently damaged.

NOT JUST A WILL, BUT A *GOOD* WILL

During the first five years of my career, I saw many of my clients wading through estate issues following the death of a parent or

---

3   Hollie Shaw, "Leon vs. Leon: Inside the Brutal Feud Tearing Apart the Furniture Dynasty," Calgary Herald, April 20, 2018, https://calgaryherald.com/news/retail-marketing/leon-vs-leon-inside-the-brutal-battle-tearing-apart-canadas-furniture-family/wcm/068ec4b8-1f1e-4bde-a74e-f43e230817da.

spouse. The importance of having a will—and what happens without one—became very clear to me. Dying intestate (i.e., without a will) can create a minefield of issues, yet many people elect not to have one. Sometimes they cannot decide exactly how they want their assets distributed—or they know that family members who may be unprepared to handle those assets will turn on one another. But the hard fact is that having a will is the best way to prevent the kind of family strife that now afflicts the Leon clan. And if you don't take the steps to put it in place, the government will take over your assets and distribute them according to their formula, typically not to your family's satisfaction and maybe not to its benefit.

It's crucial to keep in mind, though, that even if you have a will, it may not be enough. Too many wills do not address all the issues that need to be considered. Many people have intricate family relationships involving first and second spouses; children, stepchildren, and their spouses; grandchildren, step-grandchildren, and their spouses; family business succession plans; and more.

Other thorny issues include how much to leave children, and when and how to leave it so as not to create trust fund babies who may become unmotivated to work or learn or contribute to society. Many people have adult children who are not saving enough for their retirement, either because they have too many expenses and too much debt, or because they are expecting an inheritance that will support them in their golden years.[4]

It's also important to draft your will at a time when you have your full mental capacity. You don't want to wait until something happens that can result in your will being challenged (for example,

---

4   Kerri Zane, "The Shocking Reason Why Siblings Squabble Over Inheritance, and How to Prevent It," Forbes, November 14, 2016, accessed June 29, 2018, https://www.forbes.com/sites/kerrizane/2016/11/14/the-shocking-reason-why-siblings-squabble-over-inheritance-and-how-to-prevent-it/#5e95e83b64f6.

a concussion from an accident that leaves you with brain damage), or until you've reached such an advanced age that the possibility of dementia can be raised as grounds to contest the will.

While the main purpose of a will is distribution of assets, it should also serve to ensure family harmony rather than foment division and resentment. The goal is to leave stronger, more independent families when we die and are no longer there to act as tiller and rudder. I cannot emphasize enough how important it is to structure a will so that everyone feels good about the inheritance they've received and the way they've received it. This can only happen if *everything* is taken into consideration, which it all too often is not.

CHANGES

Wills should not be viewed as static. It's important to update a will every five years or anytime there's a significant development. Circumstances change, as do lifestyles, and over time we accumulate more and more wealth. Sometimes we notice that our children's capabilities have changed for the better (perhaps because a child has furthered her financial education) or for the worse (perhaps because of bankruptcy or some other personal problem). A spouse may die, or a grandchild may be born—it's even possible the executor of your will could predecease you. Any of these events would need to be taken into account to keep your will current and relevant, and family communication is crucial to the process.

WILL-ING PARTICIPANTS

When people think about creating a will, typically the first (and only) step is a visit to a lawyer's office. A lawyer takes your instructions— I'd like to leave X assets to my wife, Y money in equal amounts to my son and daughter, and Z to this charity—and drafts a legal document. But the simple act of drafting a document doesn't address the whys, hows, and wheres of a thoroughly executed will. As I said in chapter 1, the check-box mentality—going through the motions of doing something in a basic form—is a far cry from creating a comprehensive, watertight, and airtight document that covers all the bases.

The first thing I do in planning for new wills or a will update is to review the net worth statement. This allows for a more comprehensive discussion on potential strategies and opportunities available both today and in the future. Perhaps the estate will not be able to use all the tax credits available and we should start reducing taxes today. What is the composition and ownership of the assets? Where are they located—in Canada or outside the country? We have a big discussion about the family tree, including whom in your life you may be helping financially, and whom you may expect to have to help—children in college, aging parents, etc. If you're supporting an elderly parent, does that support need to continue if you predecease them, or is there another mechanism in place?

If a couple is leaving money only to each other, is the money to be left outright, or are there handcuffs—protective features which can take the form of various strategies—that need to be put on it should a new spouse or special caregiver come into the picture? What part is allocated to the children? How much is too much or too little? Do there need to be handcuffs on any of that as well—as in a trust or tranches—and if so, for what period of time? At the age of majority, a child will automatically receive all the money designated for him or her unless another plan has been put in place.

If you and your spouse die when your children are young, who will be their guardian, and what will the financial plan look like? Does the guardian have the same net worth as you? Will there be a guardian allowance—and does it need to be receipted or not? (In other words, is it necessary for the guardian to get a receipt every time he or she takes your child out for ice cream? Or perhaps expenditures need to be categorized as major or minor.) Will your children's education or lifestyle need to be altered at all?

When preparing a will, you need to keep going deeper and deeper: What if this happens and what if that happens? And then what if something else happens as a result? I generally have a big whiteboard in the office at the first couple of meetings. On that whiteboard we write Mom and Dad's names and the names of all the children and grandchildren. Then we indicate exactly where all the money is flowing, and we try to think through all the possible contingencies and variables. Anything and everything must be considered, analyzed, dissected, and further analyzed when preparing a will: lifestyle, family members, values, and what needs to be perpetuated and what let go.

While there are exceptions, most standard attorney-drawn wills are about ten or twelve pages. Our wills, however, once the lawyer has drafted our discussions, can be in the vicinity of twenty to forty pages, and sometimes there are even eighty-page wills. One reason for this is that we work with a lot of American energy-industry professionals who have moved to Canada for work. Drawing up a will for someone in this situation requires consultation with both Canadian and US lawyers, because the US has estate taxes while Canada has none.

For Canadians who own property in Canada or the US (or anywhere else in the world), it is necessary to determine how important it is to the family as a legacy, and whether it should be bequeathed to children and grandchildren. If a trust will be involved, we need to determine how it is actually going to be funded over the years. If the property is to be left to the children to own and maintain, and they have very different incomes—let's say one is an executive and the other an artist—how will that be handled?

Philanthropy is another area with a million facets. What is the appropriate amount of money to leave to charity? If it's a large amount, the client can lose many charitable tax credits, because when you die, these credits are limited to certain amounts in the year of the death and the years preceding it. This leads us into the conversation about giving some money away now, as charitable tax credits can decrease income tax while we are still alive and enable us to actually see the benefits of our philanthropy. Giving away money before you die is also a way of teaching the next generation how to manage money.

TRANSPARENCY, TODAY AND TOMORROW

Consistent communication is necessary in order to pave the way for a smooth transition when someone passes away. For instance, if you talk directly only to your children and they relay those discussions to their spouses, the latter are going to get the information secondhand. Integrating everyone into the ongoing discussion about distribution of wealth can mean the difference between war and peace—addressing and resolving conflict before it has the potential to explode and divide family members. Why has one of the children been named executor and trustee and not another? Perhaps yet another child or relative has thoughts to contribute but has not been given the opportunity to be part of the process.

Open discussion doesn't have to take the form of a big, formal meeting (unless you want it to). It can happen quietly at family gatherings or while driving in the car. What's important is that everyone is aware of what's going on and has been made to feel included in the decision-making process.

FINAL CURTAIN

Whenever we plan for a will, we also make sure we do a personal directive. This covers health-care decisions in the event that you are unable to make them yourself. We also insist that the client designate someone to have power of attorney for financial decisions. Those two documents answer a number of important questions: Who will be in charge, and for how long? Is this individual making decisions about where you will live (i.e., in a skilled nursing home as opposed to another type of facility) and the level of care you will receive? Is your money going to be used to make you as comfortable as possible, even if it significantly depletes your estate?

A will should preserve and even improve relationships, and the process of creating one should engender good feelings about the decisions you are making. There should be harmony rather than discord over the distribution of your assets. This can only be achieved when people understand how and why you are making the decisions you are making.

Chapter 7

FOMO:
FEAR OF MISSING OUT!

The term FOMO may sound more like an infectious disease than an acronym, and *fear of missing out* is indeed a condition that can permeate every cell and every aspect of our lives. It can affect the way we think and thereby affect the actions we take.

Sensational news grabs hold of us and doesn't let go. Sensational headlines want us to rush into the market, or to buy specific stocks. Headlines such as "Market Peaking—Crash Imminent" make us sit up and want to rush to get out of the market ASAP. Fear sells newspapers and stimulates clicks.

Add to that the fact that most of us are not isolated. In the urban jungle, we live and function in tribal communities—clusters of family, friends, or even friends on social media. We are not alone; it's not in our nature. Sociologists tell us that we need to feel a sense of belonging to a group, so when we hear that someone has struck it rich on a marijuana stock or bitcoin, we can't help but ask, "What about me? What's wrong with me? How did I miss out?" We are always

Prudent investing requires due diligence, careful decision-making, and a commitment to ride out the ebb and flow of the economy and **IGNORE SENSATIONAL HEADLINES** comparing ourselves to others; it's the way we're wired. Unfortunately, those feelings of needing to connect may send us scurrying to find the next big thing. We surely don't want to miss out *this* time. Consequently, when it comes to money, we can easily be drawn to fads and mired in a minefield of investment speculation.

Possibly one of the very first examples of an economic fad and the manic behavior that results from fear of missing out was in the seventeenth century. "Tulip mania," which some accounts consider the first recorded speculative bubble, took hold in 1634, during what is known today as the Dutch Golden Age. Largely based on increasing demand for the coveted bulb from other parts of Europe, particularly France, the Dutch created a type of formal futures market in which contracts to buy tulip bulbs at the end of the season were bought and sold. Contract prices skyrocketed, and then collapsed in 1637.

Prudent, thoughtful investing is not a scheme to get rich quick. A tree can be thought of as a company, with the apples on the tree being analogous to stock dividends. Just as a tree doesn't produce anything when you first plant it, an investment portfolio may not generate the dividends you want when you start out with it. It takes time and patience for it to grow and mature—for the returns to come in. But our society is infected with an ever-rising sense of urgency—the fear of missing out. We don't want to wait. We're not interested in cultivating anything long term. We want it fast. We want to get rich *now*.

Get-rich-quick schemes are a good way to get poor quick. If you want sizzle and volatility, you can go to Las Vegas and gamble—just as people gamble by investing in increasingly unstable companies like Global Crossings (more on that later). There's a difference between investing and speculating. Prudent investing requires due diligence, careful decision-making, and a commitment to ride out the ebb and flow of the economy and ignore sensational headlines.

TIME, NOT TIMING

According to a Putnam Investments report of S&P 500 Index findings from the period of December 31, 2002 through December 31, 2017, "Time, not timing, is the best way to capitalize on stock market gains. By trying to predict the best time to buy and sell, you may miss the market's biggest gains. By staying fully invested (during that fifteen-year period), you would have earned $20,460 more than someone who missed the market's ten best days."[5]

Trying to time the market can be a slippery slope. People jump in or jump out, or are fearful of getting in or getting out, or do not take the time to prudently and thoughtfully get in or get out. Sometimes people make poor decisions about these things because they don't have an established relationship with a trusted advisor, or because they lack experience with the market. Speculating about the "next big thing" because of fear of missing out only serves to complicate this.

Seasoned investors understand that, with rare exceptions, "next big thing" companies overwhelmingly do not make for the best investment opportunities. If you want to speculate, take your "play" money—whatever you can afford to lose—and go to Vegas. Your odds of getting rich are the same, and Vegas is a lot more fun! At

---

5   Putnam Investments, "Time, not timing, is the best way to capitalize on stock market gains," accessed July 17, 2019, https://www.putnam.com/literature/pdf/11508.pdf.

least when you've lost all your money at a casino, you've probably had a fun trip in other respects. The bottom line is that speculating—wherever and however you do it—is largely about dumb luck.

TALK ABOUT A REVOLUTION

Remember the dot-com bubble of the 1990s? That era was rife with speculation. The internet was going to revolutionize the world—and, of course, it *has* revolutionized the world—but most of the companies formed at that time have not survived. A company called Global Crossings was going to lay all the fiber optics underneath the ocean—the process that would facilitate the internet. No one imagined a company like that could ever fail! But Global Crossings never had a profitable year,[6] and it went bankrupt in 2002.[7] Lots of technology stocks went belly-up in those days, and lots of investors lost their shirts. The problem is that many people fail to perform due diligence before investing; they don't take a good, hard look at the company—its income statements, balance sheets, its overall performance and profitability. They just want to strike while the iron is hot.

Similar stories abound: Blackberry was a successful start-up company until it was surpassed by Apple, and then it wasn't successful. Of course, many young companies defy the odds, but as a rule, speculating by investing in them is equivalent to shooting craps in Las Vegas. People become enamored of a company that supposedly is going to radically change the world, and their fear of missing out takes hold. But taking the time to thoroughly dissect and analyze a company's performance before jumping in can make an immense

---

6   Timothy L. O'Brien, "A New Legal Chapter for a 90's Flameout," *New York Times*, August 15, 2004.

7   Christopher Stern, "Global Crossing Files for Bankruptcy," *Washington Post*, January 29, 2002.

difference. We use professional money managers whose job it is to analyze the companies in our clients' portfolios so that clients don't make mistakes over fear of missing out. Most people aren't capable of properly analyzing a company on their own and comparing it to other opportunities in a disciplined process—that's why DIY investors don't ever really make money.

EGGS IN THE RIGHT BASKETS

Earlier in this book we talked about the fear of running out of money in retirement. In order to prevent that eventuality, investments must be made thoughtfully, with due diligence, and then given time to grow and mature. Though times have changed, many of the same things that motivated people in the time of tulip mania continue to motivate us today: having enough to eat and keeping a roof over our heads until the day we die, living well until that day, and if possible providing something for our families and to make the world a better place after we are gone.

In the pursuit of these goals, sometimes we have to guard against our own behavior, against human nature—against fear of missing out. My client Owen came to me during the dot-com era with a concentrated position in a high-flying technology stock. He was making a lot of money on the stock because it was moving. I recommended selling it all because I didn't like the complexion of the company, but the client didn't sell. Fortunately, the stock did not make up his entire portfolio (we don't like to see more than 5 percent of your portfolio in one particular company), because he lost all the money he'd invested in it. As many people who experience this kind of loss do, he then had to undertake the task of trying to earn back all of that money through other investments. It took a very long time.

Gina, another client, was a midlevel executive at a large start-up technology company, making a great deal of money. It was 1998, and the company was going full bore—and she was heavily invested in its stock. Every time a stock option would cross her desk, she thought she was richer. Although her stock was growing by leaps and bounds, I tried to impress upon her that no one should have an entire portfolio invested in any single company, much less a start-up. There is just too much risk. Finally she deferred to my experience, and over a period of six months, she sold all of her company stock so we could build her a much more stable and conservative retirement income portfolio. The company ended up in bankruptcy; had she kept going the way she was, she would have had absolutely nothing to retire with.

GOOD AND BAD = NOT GOOD

Another way financial institutions feed upon people's fear of missing out is with what they call "structured products"—a new way of investing. The subprime mortgage crisis that occurred between 2007 and 2010 is an example of this kind of investment, and we know what happened there. Banks sold mortgage portfolios, packaging good mortgages with bad, but all of them were rated as good mortgages. The fallout was a massive component of the Great Recession.

There are also tax schemes that people get into in hopes of reducing their taxes. Flow-through shares, or FTSs, related to the energy industry, are one of those vehicles. But an investment decision should be driven by the product, not the prospect of tax savings. Again, people don't always take the time to analyze what they're investing in. FTSs help raise capital for exploration and project development activities, and they promise tax savings; however, they may not be good investments, and if they are, the underlying common stock is often a better value.

ONCE AND NOT AGAIN

Stock speculation is one expression of fear of missing out, but speculation takes other forms as well. We had a client who'd built his own oil and gas company—a private company that he successfully took public, earning himself a very big payday in the process. We then diversified his portfolio, and it was a beautiful thing for him and us to see the results!

But then another investment opportunity came along, and against our advice, he went out and borrowed against his portfolio to invest in another energy company. He thought, "You know what? It was easy the first time. I can do this again." But the investment went bad, and in the end, while he was able to keep his home, he lost all of his money because of factors beyond his control, such as the price of oil.

People think if they have the right idea or the right company, and they've done it before, they will win again. But most of the time it doesn't work that way. One of my mantras is *never put your retirement at risk*. If you want to invest in another company and have the funds to do so, go right ahead. But risking the money you've set aside for your retirement is never wise.

The first time they venture out with a big product or idea, most entrepreneurs are at least a decade or two younger than they are the next time they take that plunge. There is still risk, but the risk is a lot lower at an earlier stage in life. The first time around my client had mortgaged his house and used his and his wife's retirement savings. He was all in on the business, and his future depended on whether it lived or died. That's the entrepreneurial spirit, and who are any of us to discourage entrepreneurship? But being all in the second time around can have serious repercussions. You have much more at stake, and if you lose it, you are likely in your fifties or sixties, with much less time to build it back up—if that's even possible.

Our culture wants us to want more. We want more for ourselves. We want more for our families, and we can view money as protection. It's human nature to be out looking for the next big thing, but that's not always the best thing to do. In fact it rarely is.

Chapter 8

IF YOU DON'T PAY FOR A PLAN, IT'S WORTHLESS

There's a psychology behind valuing what we pay for—what we invest in—above what we don't. There may be times in your life when you've received a gift, and while it was nice, somehow it didn't occupy the same place in your thoughts as something you'd saved for and purchased on your own. Or perhaps when you were younger and starting out, someone gave you a used piece of furniture or another object for your apartment because they were remodeling their home and it no longer fit their design plan. But it was not a purchase you made yourself, and over time, you may not have regarded it in the same way you would have had you invested your own money in it. The same psychology is used by animal welfare groups that require an adoption fee for a pet. Besides needing to offset their costs, they require this fee because they know that if you invest money in a pet, you are more likely to continue to invest time, energy, and resources in that pet's care.

We are no different in our thinking about the fees we charge for the kind of financial planning we do. Most firms earn their money strictly through investment management, by taking a percentage based on the amount of assets invested, which is something we do as well. But we have a different philosophy when it comes to all the services we provide.

In the last ten or so years, financial professionals have finally started thinking about their clients' actual long-term goals for the money they invest—the big picture—as opposed to simply picking the right stocks. Long-range planning is a huge expenditure of time and effort, and in the past it wasn't that common. Even today, few people go to the great lengths we do to dissect and analyze every single component of your life in order to arrive at the optimal plan.

When I started practicing in 1998, my role was essentially to choose stocks and bonds for people. But as I've stated throughout the book, financial planning is about much more than that. I maintain an ongoing dialogue with clients about their money from the very beginning of our relationship and over months and years, and doing this has opened my eyes to the amount of time and effort it takes for my team and me to maintain a high level of in-depth and ongoing service.

Many people still seem to subscribe to the check-box mentality; they believe they can use one-size-fits-all software to plan their financial future on their own. Even the financial advisors I've met don't always seem to engage in the in-depth planning we do, which takes a significant amount of research and strategizing. While some of the same thinking may apply to choosing the right stocks for people (not an easy process by any means), a lifelong financial plan requires you to do more. You are touching on every aspect of people's lives, drawing out their values, goals, wishes, and hopes for their families.

It takes a different kind of thinking to successfully integrate all the pieces of someone's financial life. Then we need to make sure the client actually understands and accepts our advice and implements it. It's not a common skill set, and it took me years to hone and master it. Many advisors are giving it away for free, so to speak, and earning a living strictly from investment management, because they're not putting the necessary time into comprehensive planning.

When we sit down with a client at that pivotal first meeting, so much is required of the client in terms of gathering materials for our purposes that we've found that a monetary investment is a great incentive for them to collect *all* of those materials. The gathering of materials that may be stored in various places and at different institutions, some not thought about for years, can be daunting to contemplate, and actually doing it is tedious. The fee we charge is a motivator.

Before we began charging for our financial planning services in 2011, we found that busy clients sometimes took months to gather the material we needed to do our jobs. Now we've found that clients who paid that fee were not only more willing to do that work, but also more inclined to be open and transparent in important conversations with us—which, as I've said before, can be difficult. With a fee there was a higher level of engagement—or in sports vernacular, more skin in the game. Again, the psychological effect is that investing in something equals more effort put into making it work.

ON THE OTHER SIDE OF THE DESK

Once we started charging, the quality of the financial plans *we* produced was better. It's not that we hadn't always given 150 percent to our clients, but just as charging the client worked to motivate him or her, it provided a better incentive for us as well, from a psy-

> You cannot get to where you need to be without appropriate investment management and

INTEGRATION OF EVERYTHING

chological standpoint. It's human nature for us to want to be paid for the hard work we do. That applies to any profession. What's more, the question of what and how to charge caused us to take a look at the way we managed our practice, the resources we used, and all the services and processes we performed. How could we make them even better for the client?

None of this is to say we don't earn money on the investment management side of our firm. Of course we do. But we cannot competently invest funds without the financial planning tie-in—the big picture. In the past we've found that if we isolate the plan from actual investment management, the plan doesn't come to fruition because management of the funds is not done properly or not rebalanced or not reviewed on a regular basis. We cannot count on the plan succeeding. It doesn't sync up. Funds are not properly diversified and risk is not properly accounted for unless we steer the ship. You cannot get to where you need to be without appropriate investment management and integration of *everything*. Often a new client will come to us because they don't like the way their portfolio is performing or they are unhappy with their advisor. They come to us strictly for investment management, in their minds something urgent, but we have to switch that conversation around and explain that we're not even going to look at their investments until they let us work out a plan with them. Planning is at the core of what we do, and this results in clients being much better served.

THE JOURNEY

The plan we will ultimately create involves anywhere from forty to one hundred hours of work. At our first meeting, we explain our policy: We will not work with you unless we do a personalized, comprehensive financial plan—not just investment management. If you have some kind of a plan already in place—which has been the case only twice in my more-than-twenty-year career—we ask that you bring it to the first meeting. (Even if you have a plan, chances are it's been sitting on a shelf somewhere, gathering dust for years, with nothing put into action.) We also get copies of your tax returns and all of your account statements, life insurance and critical illness documentation, and disability insurance information. We use an expense worksheet, or if you have some idea of your expenses, you can bring in the figures on paper or email us a spreadsheet

We need to see your assets, and you need to come prepared to tell us the value of all of your assets—how much you paid for your home; what vacation and/or rental properties you own; how much you owe on everything; what the interest rates are. We need to find out what you are paying for all that debt. Assets and liabilities. Tax returns. We need it all.

We also do a family tree, which is fairly easy, and we require all of your personal planning documents, including a will, trust information, power of attorney, advance directive, etc.

Work-related information is important: items such as pension statements or group retirement savings accounts at work, partnership agreements, and the like.

When all of this is brought to the first meeting (which typically lasts ninety minutes but can go as long as two and a half hours), we make sure we have what we need in place, but then it's immediately put aside for the bigger conversation about values, family issues, retirement goals, etc. Then we examine everything meaningful to you.

When all is said and done, we send a follow-up e-mail summarizing what occurred in the first meeting. We then spend two weeks poring over everything; reaching out to bankers, lawyers, and/or accountants if something is missing; synthesizing everything; and aligning what we have with the client's long-term goals. At that point, we will create a comprehensive financial plan that is easily thirty or forty pages. It will cover investment management and address any pressing concerns we may have right out of the starting gate, based on the materials given to us for this purpose. The plan will also dig deep into estate planning, as many clients come to us with deficiencies in that area—incomplete or obsolete documents, or no documents whatsoever. The particulars are acutely important here: who is going to raise my child, how and where is she going to be raised, who will acquire my pets, and all the other crucial details described throughout this book.

When we address investments, we make it clear we that do not buy stocks and bonds ourselves. This is something I used to do but not now. We outsource that task to pension fund managers who run the Canada Pension Plan or Canada Post Pension Plan or other big pension plans in Canada. We are very precise when we talk about how the client's money is going to be managed, however, and it may take a month or so for his or her assets to be transferred from another firm. When we have everything in place, we have a second meeting to go over the entire plan.

The plan's implementation phase takes anywhere from twelve to eighteen months. We meet quarterly or more often during that time to make sure we're on track.

In the area of estate planning, we may need two or three meetings with a lawyer before all of it is done. If we are setting up a charitable foundation, we may require two or three meetings to put it in place. If setting up a family trust, we may bring in a tax lawyer, and sometimes that in itself requires multiple meetings.

As I've mentioned before, about 10 percent of Calgarians are US citizens. As well as US citizens, we may be dealing with citizens of multiple countries who may have properties around the world. Because of that, we need to bring in a cross-border tax specialist to handle all the intricate details of the Canadian and other countries tax treaties and estate laws. We are good at what we do, but we do not profess to be authorities in everything. In those instances, we make sure you understand that you will incur the extra fees, which will be paid directly to an outside expert. But we manage and monitor the entire process with meetings held at our offices. The results of these meetings go out to you in follow-up emails or in-person meetings, along with our advice based on your goals and values. We then integrate the results into the long-term financial plan.

Sometimes what we offer is just the advice of the sobering second voice. For example, Bill, a senior level executive, came to us with an interesting question. He had heard tax rates were less expensive in some states in the US versus Canada where he and his family lived, so was considering a move to the US. He wanted to know what would be involved in changing his residency. While we called in experts to verify what he'd heard about the respective tax rates of various states and across Canada, and the necessary steps to change residency, we also had multiple conversations with him during which he said repeatedly that all of his and his wife's friends and the rest of their family were in Canada. So we asked him, "Is it worth giving up all that to start over at this time in your life, just to save a certain amount of tax? Just how important is money compared to the life you and your family have built?" Only the client can make a decision like that, but that objective second voice is something we frequently provide. We are always interested in building relationships with our clients, and that requires open, honest communication.

REVIEW AND REPEAT

My team and I meet with every client according to their needs, typically quarterly, to review their portfolio with them and make any adjustments to their plan or to their portfolio. Major life changes happen during the time between these meetings, and we stay involved. Perhaps we need to update a will now and then because of changes in the makeup of a family—death, divorce, etc. But even if there are no such changes, the will is routinely updated about every five years.

Every year we update the core financial plan. Thinking about tax planning is something we do consistently throughout the year. Clients receive a paycheck of sorts for expenses every month, and generally around November we'll do an analysis of their tax situation on their investment portfolio, looking at how much tax they've paid to date. Maybe we can trigger capital gains because they are not taking advantage of all the tax deductions they could be. Or maybe we want to invoke capital losses. We may look at charitable giving at that time of year in order to reduce the tax bill and certainly to fund worthy causes close to the client's heart. Year-end tax planning is paramount at this time of year.

Everything we do involves an inordinate amount of hard work, expertise, and time. There are better stock pickers and investment managers than me, and we do our own due diligence in selecting best-in-class investment managers to interface with you. There is a reason we don't do it all ourselves. As wealth advisors, outsourcing to other experts when necessary gives us the time and energy to focus full-time on the best planning we can possibly do for each and every client. Who says the wealthy are ill-served? Certainly not here.

Chapter 9

AN INVITATION TO CONTINUE THE CONVERSATION

If you like what you've read so far, are a senior executive or business owner, or are nearing retirement or are in any of life's many transition points and have been wondering if we are a good fit for one another, I ask you to consider the following.

While diverse experiences and specific financial planning goals vary among our clients, most have one thing in common: They are used to delegating. Inherent in working with our team is the idea that you need to be comfortable leaving the driving to us, as the old advertisement says. If you are a high-net-worth businessperson, chances are you are just as competent transferring some decision-making responsibilities to other experts—recognized in their respective fields—as you are in your own decision-making. Probably you are at or near the top of your profession and have spent some challenging years getting there. You've made all kinds of choices and decisions about people along the way. As such you recognize that different skill sets may be needed to achieve real success in a field that isn't yours. That's where we come in. In brief, our best client is one who is comfortable identifying the best wealth advisors in the field and confidently delegating the job to us.

We also appreciate prospective clients who come to us at a time of transition. Money may be in motion if you are selling the business, or thinking of selling the business, or if you are exploring succession planning. You could own either a large or small business and be transitioning in this way.

Also in the realm of transitions, perhaps you are getting married for the first or second time, going through a divorce, starting a family, or blending one. Transitions are good catalysts and make for the kinds of clients that work well with our strategies and ideas. Life-altering situations cause people to step back and think hard about what they want and need, which makes us better able to work with you.

Highly noteworthy is the fact that we excel at strategic philanthropy. Advisors may shy away from this area of planning because it may cannibalize their business. If a client gives away a million dollars to charity, that impacts the advisor's business, as those assets are removed from their management for years to come. We are confident that by doing right by the client and the charity, those assets will come back to us tenfold.

IT TAKES TWO

Next, if you are considering working with us, we strongly recommend that if you have a significant other—a partner or spouse, or if you are in a common-law marriage, or if you simply have someone else with whom you are sharing your life—that individual needs to be present during the financial planning process. Though it sometimes happens that one person in the relationship makes all the financial decisions, if you're that person who does not bring in your partner, then we can't do the job for you. The reason is we only end up hearing half of the life goals, dreams (and fears and motivations), and everything else, which does not provide for a thorough job or even the right kind of job.

When we have our introductory meeting, we're fine meeting with half a unit, so to speak. But when we start our discovery meeting, we need to have both of you there because it's all about your life together. We're going to be talking in great detail about how you both want to spend your time and where you want to spend it, essentially where you want to wake up in the morning for the rest of your lives. What does that feel like? Look like? In fact, if we're getting into the fine details, what does it smell like? Is it a morning walk through Versailles' fragrant gardens or maybe strong coffee brewing as owners of your own country bed-and-breakfast? Are you going to stay close to home, join multiple boards, and/or start a foundation? And how do you think your mind and health will be impacted by this major decision affecting the rest of your lives? It's impossible to take these kinds of steps without input from both involved parties.

We put dollars and figures around your ideas ... if you want to be on Spain's Costa Brava three months of the year and then you want to take your children and grandchildren skiing each year for Christmas, how much is all that going to cost? Can you really do it? We need both of you there, even if you're the one primarily making the decisions. Each of you must understand, firsthand, both the asset and spending sides of the ledger and feel happy about and comfortable with your decisions.

ACROSS THE DESK

When you contact us, we typically respond by saying we would like to have a twenty-to-thirty-minute conversation. We prefer that you come to us, because we always find it is best meeting people face-to-face. We are about to help you figure out the rest of your life, and so much of any important relationship is how comfortable we are with one another. There is no obligation, and at that point we're just going to talk a little bit about what we do and find out something about your situation, including whether you are open to suggestions and delegating. This will help us determine whether we fit together well.

Maybe we will have two or three introductory meetings, depending on your time and questions, before you are ready to come on board and progress to the discovery meeting. We'll also look at the investment management component with you, and I cannot emphasize enough that it is never our intention to pass judgment over past actions you may have taken in the financial arena. As accomplished as people are, there is that element of human nature where they don't necessarily want to hold themselves up to the light. They are not interested in subjecting themselves to the kind of judgment that may result from intense scrutiny. Respectfully, we're not interested in that either. We only wish to go forward in providing the best future for you, and we want you to be sure we've left no stone unturned in providing a solid financial blueprint for the rest of your lives.

Ready to get started? So are we! We're eager to welcome you to the Susan O'Brien Group.

CPSIA information can be obtained
at www.ICGtesting.com
Printed in the USA
LVHW080526090120
642850LV00001BA/1/P